Heather E. Schwartz

CAPSTONE PRESS
a capstone imprint

Published by Capstone Press, an imprint of Capstone
1710 Roe Crest Drive
North Mankato, Minnesota 56003
capstonepub.com

Copyright © 2026 by Capstone. All rights reserved. No part of this publication may be reproduced in whole or in part, or stored in a retrieval system, or transmitted in any form or by any means, electronic, mechanical, photocopying, recording, or otherwise, without written permission of the publisher.

Library of Congress Cataloging-in-Publication Data is available on the Library of Congress website.

ISBN: 9798875228285 (hardcover)
ISBN: 9798875232084 (paperback)
ISBN: 9798875232091 (ebook PDF)

Summary: The world is an amazing place. Natural wonders, like black sand beaches and white rainbows, and human-made achievements, like skyscrapers and technology, are just waiting to be explored! Bright pictures, humorous designs, and amazing facts will invite readers to appreciate the wonders of the world.

Editorial Credits
Editor: Mari Bolte; Designer: Kay Fraser;
Media Researcher: Svetlana Zhurkin;
Production Specialist: Katy LaVigne

Image Credits
Alamy: Imago/WWF/Thy Neang, 29; Capstone: Kay Fraser (design elements), cover and throughout; Getty Images: Anton Aleksenko, cover (bottom left), 27, David Madison, cover (moai), Jiri Anderle, 9, mikroman6, 25, Peter Zelei Images, 13, Ron and Patty Thomas, 31; Shutterstock: 6DecPhotographer, 20, ajborges, 11, Altug Galip, 12, Andrew Ring, 19, Blueee77, 26, Declan Hillman, 24, frank_peters, 18, Imfoto, 23, Jeremy Richards, 16, kavram, 15, Marius Sipa Photography, 6, marketa1982, 28, matthieu Gallet, cover (bottom right), 5 (bottom), Milon Khondaker, 30, n_widyo utomo, 17, NikolajPovlsen, 14, picturepixx (Colosseum), cover, 21, Poorty Chitre, 10, SCStock, 5 (top), Somchai Som, 22, Stephen Bonk, 7, YuniqueB, 8

Any additional websites and resources referenced in this book are not maintained, authorized, or sponsored by Capstone. All product and company names are trademarks™ or registered® trademarks of their respective holders.

Printed and bound in the USA. 6307

TABLE OF CONTENTS

CHAPTER 1
WEIRDEST WONDERS 4

CHAPTER 2
NATURAL WONDERS 10

CHAPTER 3
HUMAN-MADE WONDERS 18

CHAPTER 4
MYSTERIES: SOLVED AND UNSOLVED 24

CHAPTER 1
WEIRDEST WONDERS

Want to explore the wonders of the world? Check out these awe-inspiring lists of amazing sights, sounds, and mysteries on Earth—and beyond!

STRANGE SOUNDS

- Earth's hum—a continuous pulsing note too low for humans to hear
- The Bloop—rumbles of underwater icequakes deep in the ocean
- Singing sand—squeaks, booms, and roars caused by wind over dunes

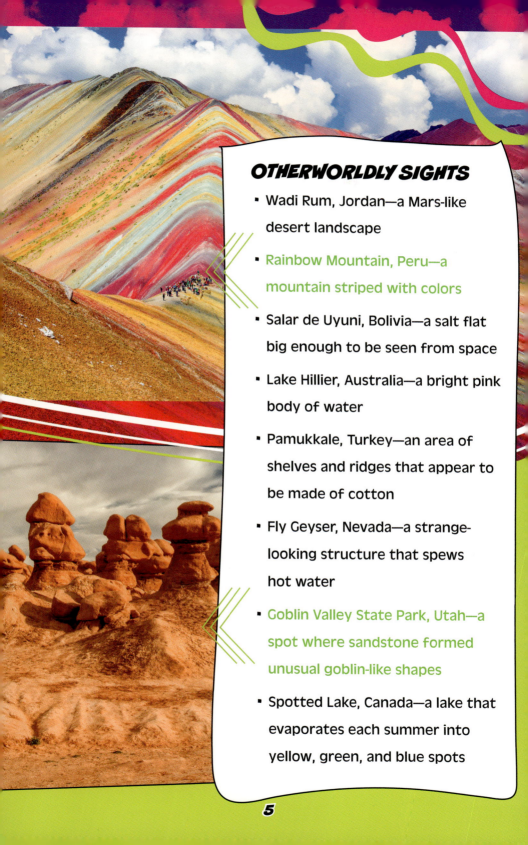

OTHERWORLDLY SIGHTS

- Wadi Rum, Jordan—a Mars-like desert landscape
- Rainbow Mountain, Peru—a mountain striped with colors
- Salar de Uyuni, Bolivia—a salt flat big enough to be seen from space
- Lake Hillier, Australia—a bright pink body of water
- Pamukkale, Turkey—an area of shelves and ridges that appear to be made of cotton
- Fly Geyser, Nevada—a strange-looking structure that spews hot water
- Goblin Valley State Park, Utah—a spot where sandstone formed unusual goblin-like shapes
- Spotted Lake, Canada—a lake that evaporates each summer into yellow, green, and blue spots

SECRETIVE SPOTS

- North Sentinel Island, India—home of the Sentinelese tribe and off-limits to visitors
- Coca-Cola vault, Georgia—a safe place for the secret formula
- Area 51, Nevada—a desert Air Force base linked to alien life
- Greenbrier Resort Bunker, West Virginia—an underground bunker large enough to hold all 535 members of Congress

WONDERS BEYOND THE WORLD

No telescope is needed to view these outer space sights!

- The Moon
- Jupiter
- International Space Station
- Milky Way Galaxy
- Orion Nebula

ISLANDS FULL OF ANIMALS

Some islands have more animals than people!

- Cat Island, Japan—It has six times more cats than people!
- Monkey Island, Puerto Rico—1,500 monkeys call this island home.
- Pig Beach, Bahamas—People visit from all over the world to swim with the wild pigs.
- Okunoshima Island, Japan—This island has 30 times more rabbits than people!
- Macquarie Island, Australia—3.5 million royal, king, and rockhopper penguins live here.
- Kauai, Hawaii—More than 450,000 chickens roam the island. That's six chickens for every person who lives there!
- Assateague Island, Maryland—Every year, a herd of horses swims from Assateague to nearby Chincoteague Island.

OUT-OF-PLACE ART

- Cadillac Ranch, Texas—a collection of 10 cars half-planted in the ground
- *Hand of the Desert,* Chile—a 36-foot- (11-meter-) tall concrete sculpture stretching from sand to sky
- Prada Marfa, Texas—a building designed as a fake fashion shop in the middle of a desert
- Noah Purifoy Outdoor Desert Art Museum, California—a collection of sculptures created from junk
- *Desert Breath,* Egypt—land art in the shape of a double-spiral
- *Moon Phases,* the Moon—125 miniature sculptures of the moon placed there by the *Odysseus* lander

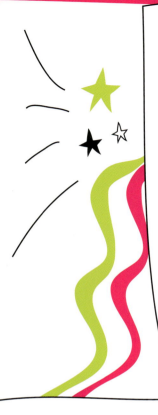

ANIMAL IMITATORS

- Tree ocelots mimic monkey sounds.
- Spicebush swallowtail caterpillars disguise themselves as bird droppings.
- Viceroy butterflies look like toxic monarch butterflies.
- Alligator snapping turtles have a tongue that looks like a worm.
- The elephant hawk-moth caterpillar's markings make it look like a snake.
- The mimic octopus transforms to look like a jellyfish, crab, stingray, or sea snake.

IT'S ALIVE!

- Slime molds can move several feet per day to find food.
- Oyster mushrooms poison and paralyze tiny creatures called nematodes. Then they dissolve the nematode bodies and absorb them.
- Zombie-ant fungus infects carpenter ants. It slowly takes over the ant's brain!
- More than 70 species of fungi can glow in the dark.

CHAPTER 2
NATURAL WONDERS

You might not believe it till you see it with your own eyes, so check out these beautiful, bizarre, and baffling gifts from Mother Nature!

RAINBOW-COLORED BEACHES

Not all beaches are beige! Put one of these colorful coastlines on your "someday" wish list.

- Rainbow Beach, Australia
- Glass Beach, California
- Glass Beach, Hawaii

RED SAND BEACHES

- Cavendish Beach, Canada
- Kokkini Beach, Greece
- Rábida Island, Ecuador

ORANGE SAND BEACHES

- Ramla Bay, Malta
- Porto Covo, Portugal
- Porto Ferro, Italy

GREEN SAND BEACHES

- Papakōlea Beach, Hawaii
- Talofofo Beach, Guam
- Punta Cormorant, Ecuador
- Hornindalsvatnet, Norway

PURPLE SAND BEACHES

- Pfeiffer Beach, California
- Purple Sands Beach, Canada
- Plum Island, Massachusetts

BLACK SAND BEACHES

- Punalu'u Black Sand Beach, Hawaii
- Muriwai Beach, New Zealand
- Reynisfjara Beach, Iceland

PINK SAND BEACHES

- Harbour Island, the Bahamas
- Horseshoe Bay Beach, Bermuda
- Elafonisi Beach, Greece
- Komodo Island, Indonesia

DEADLIEST TOURIST TRAPS

Watch out—danger ahead!

- Gates of Hell, Turkmenistan—a huge pit of life-threatening fire
- Naica Crystal Cave, Mexico—a cave where high heat and humidity are deadly
- Cave of Death, Costa Rica—a cave where toxic air kills all who enter
- Mont Blanc, French and Italian Alps—a high peak where around 100 climbers lose their lives each year

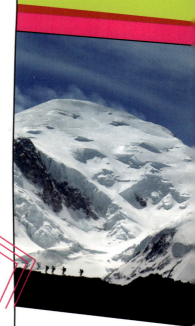

HUMANS KEEP OUT!

The animals that live on these islands have requested "no human visitors, please."

- Snake Island, Brazil—home to 4,000 endangered and venomous snakes
- Surtsey Island, Iceland—home to protected plants, animals, and soil
- North Brother Island, New York City—home to gulls, herons, and other protected birds
- Heard Island, Australia—home to seabirds, penguins, and seals

STUNNING LIGHT TRICKS

- white rainbows—arches in the sky caused by fog
- mammatus clouds—cloud pouches made of ice
- lightning sprites—red lightning created by electricity high in the sky
- Brocken spectre—a person's giant shadow cast on foggy days
- northern lights and southern lights—lights in the night sky caused by activity on the surface of the sun

QUIETEST PLACES

- Haleakalā Crater, Maui—It's so quiet that visitors can hear their own heartbeats!
- Hoh Rain Forest, Washington—This lush forest is considered to be the quietest place in the United States.
- Kelso Dune Field, California—Tall sand dunes stop sound from traveling.
- Zabalo River, Ecuador—Hours pass here without any noise.

TOP ATTRACTIONS

How many people visit every year?

- Grand Canyon, Arizona—5 million
- Moraine Lake at Banff National Park, Canada—4 million
- Ha Long Bay, Vietnam—2.6 million
- Matterhorn, Switzerland and Italy—2 million (around 3,000 try to climb it!)
- Great Barrier Reef, Australia—2 million
- Cliffs of Moher, Ireland—1.5 million
- Table Mountain, South Africa—800,000

SUPER SMALL ISLANDS

- Just Enough Room Island, New York—3,300 square feet (307 square m)
- Yap, Micronesia—38.7 square miles (100 square kilometers)
- Bishop Rock, Britain—7,922 square feet (736 square m)
- Sea Lion Island, Falkland Islands—3 square miles (7.8 square km)

ERUPTIONS AND EXPLOSIONS

- Paricutin volcano, Mexico—formed as a nine-year eruption from 1943 to 1952
- Mount Tambora volcano, Indonesia—site of the world's largest volcanic eruption, which occurred in 1815
- Mount Marapi volcano, Indonesia—very active between 1999 and 2023
- Lake Nyos, Cameroon—a deadly eruption that released tons of gas in 1986
- Biscuit Basin geyser, Wyoming—a surprising explosion of water, mud, rocks, and steam in 2024

PRETTY (AND PRETTY STRANGE) PLANTS

- bleeding hearts—red, heart-shaped flowers
- Japanese blood grass—grows as red-colored grass
- witch's hair—greenish lichen that grows in a tangled mass
- cobra lily—takes the posture of a snake about to strike
- Venus flytrap—traps and eats flies
- doll's eye—develops poisonous berries that are white with a dark dot
- ghost plant—looks spooky with its pale gray powdery coating

CHAPTER 3
HUMAN-MADE WONDERS

It's hard to improve on Mother Nature, but humans keep trying!

GIANT THINGS

Tallest Building
- Burj Khalifa, Dubai, United Arab Emirates—2,716.5 feet (828 m) tall

Longest Undersea Tunnel
- The Channel Tunnel between the island of Great Britain and mainland Europe—31.6 miles (50.9 km) long

Tallest Bridge
- Millau Viaduct, France—1,125 feet (343 m) tall

Longest Wall
- Great Wall of China—13,171 miles (21,197 km) long

TINY THINGS

They really exist—even if you can't see them!

- *Trust*, a nano sculpture smaller than the eye of a needle
- Willard Wigan's handmade sculptures that fit INSIDE a human hair
- a remote-controlled robotic crab half a millimeter wide
- world's smallest motor made of 16 atoms
- a computer smaller than a grain of salt

CONSTRUCTED ISLANDS

- Little Island, New York City—It's built on top of wood and concrete columns.
- Our Lady of the Rock, Montenegro—It's built from sunken ships and rocks.
- The Palm Jumeirah, Dubai—It's made of sand in the shape of a palm tree.

QUIETEST ROOMS

- A chamber at the Microsoft headquarters in Washington state absorbs all sounds inside.
- A chamber in Orfield Laboratories, Minnesota, is so silent you can hear yourself blink!

CHALLENGES FOR THRILL-SEEKERS

- Ride Formula Rossa, the world's fastest roller coaster, in Abu Dhabi, United Arab Emirates.
- Bungee jump off Macau Tower in China.
- Take a stroll across China's Zhangjiajie Glass Bridge.
- Climb to Tiger's Nest Monastery in Bhutan.

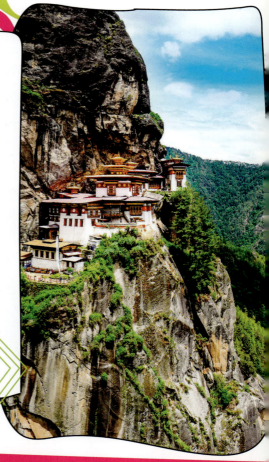

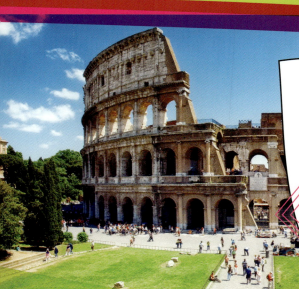

ANCIENT PLACES

- Chichén Itzá, Mexico
- Machu Picchu, Peru
- Great Stupa, Sanchi, India
- The Colosseum, Rome, Italy

SPEAK NOW

There are more than 7,000 languages spoken around the world. But there are also many invented languages that people (and fictional creatures) speak, including:

- Toki Pona—a language invented in 2001 to help people live and speak more simply—thousands of people speak it!
- Elvish—used by characters in books by J.R.R. Tolkien
- Klingon—spoken by an alien race in the Star Trek universe
- Na'vi—used in the world of *Avatar*
- Gallifreyan—used by the Time Lords in *Doctor Who*
- Lapine—spoken by rabbits in the book *Watership Down*
- Esperanto—invented to be a common language between many different people, with as many as 2 million speakers around the world!
- Alienese—used by characters in the show *Futurama*

TOP INVENTIONS

Where would we be without these innovative, world-changing inventions?

- wheel
- nail
- light bulb
- concrete
- printing press
- penicillin
- compass
- magnifying glass
- telephone
- battery

WONDERFUL WAYS TO GET AROUND

- Birds Eye Pea Car—shaped like a pea to boost vegetable sales!
- Oscar Mayer Wienermobile—a hot dog on wheels
- hovercraft—uses cushioned air to skim over water
- duck boat—a vehicle that goes on water or roads
- electric skateboard—stop and go with the press of a pedal!
- L.L. Bean Bootmobile—the fastest boot ever
- penny farthing—an early bike with a giant front wheel

CHAPTER 4
MYSTERIES: SOLVED AND UNSOLVED

The truth is out there. Or is it?

FAMOUS CRYPTIDS

- Loch Ness Monster
- Lake Champlain's Champ
- Bigfoot
- Abominable Snowman
- Will-o'-the-wisp
- Chupacabra

HAIR-RAISING RAIN

Duck and cover!

- The Kentucky Meat Shower—In 1876, meat rained from the sky over Bath County, Kentucky.
- Oakville Blobs—In 1994, jellylike blobs fell from the sky over Oakville, Washington.
- Blood Rain—when red desert dust in the air makes rain look like blood
- Spider Rain—when millions of spiders take flight all at once using silk web "parachutes"
- Fish Rain—Some tornadoes can scoop up fish and then drop them later.
- Frog Rain—Tornadoes can carry frogs too!

LOST TREASURE

- Ark of the Covenant—a storage chest for religious relics missing since around 600 BCE
- Montezuma's Treasure—Aztec gold lost in the 16th century
- Blackbeard's Treasure—a fortune in stolen pirate's booty, lost since the 1700s
- Treasure of Lima—buried treasure lost in Peru in 1820
- Mosby's Treasure—gold, silver, jewelry, and more missing in Virginia since 1863

UNANSWERED QUESTIONS

- Where is Queen Cleopatra's Tomb?
- Was King Arthur real?
- What happened to the Roanoke colony?
- What does the Voynich Manuscript say?
- What happened to Amelia Earhart?
- Does Atlantis exist?

STRANGE DESIGNS

- Nazca Lines, Peru
- Crop circles, southern England
- Paracas Candelabra, Peru
- The Eye of the Sahara, Mauritania

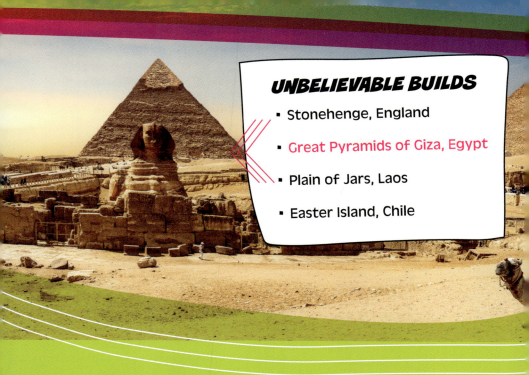

UNBELIEVABLE BUILDS

- Stonehenge, England
- Great Pyramids of Giza, Egypt
- Plain of Jars, Laos
- Easter Island, Chile

MYSTERIOUS LIGHTS

- Marfa Lights—Mysterious orbs move and change color near Marfa, Texas.
- atmospheric halos—Light plus atmospheric ice crystals create arcs and circles in the sky.
- blue blobs—A combination of lightning and light from the Moon creates orbs that hang over the Gulf of Thailand and near the South China Sea.

TROUBLING TRIANGLES

- The Michigan Triangle, Lake Michigan—site of shipwrecks, plane crashes, and disappearances
- The Dragon's Triangle, near the Japanese coast—haunted by ghost ships and sea monsters
- The Bridgewater Triangle, southeastern Massachusetts—home to giant snakes, ghosts, and Bigfoot-like creatures
- The Bermuda Triangle, north Atlantic Ocean—where aircraft and ships mysteriously disappear

SPOOKY SPOTS

- Blood Falls, Antarctica—iron in the water colors it red
- Crooked Forest, Poland—400 weirdly shaped pine trees
- Whale Bone Alley, Siberia, Russia—hundreds of whale bones that stick out of the ground
- The Island of the Dolls, Mexico—world's largest collection of creepy dolls

NEW DISCOVERIES IN THE 2020s

- 2024—Seven new species of tree frogs were discovered.
- 2023—A bright blue tarantula that can control light with its body hairs was discovered in Thailand.
- 2022—The southern maned sloth was discovered. Its head is shaped like a coconut!
- 2021—Rice's whale was discovered. There are only about 50 surviving whales.
- 2020—503 new species were discovered worldwide—like this frog!

UNEXPLORED AREAS

There are still places on Earth that are mysteries. We know they're there—but that's all we know!

- 95 percent of the universe!
- parts of Greenland hidden under miles of ice
- the deepest part of the Pacific Ocean, the Mariana Trench
- parts of Antarctica
- the summit of Mount Gangkhar Puensum, Tibet

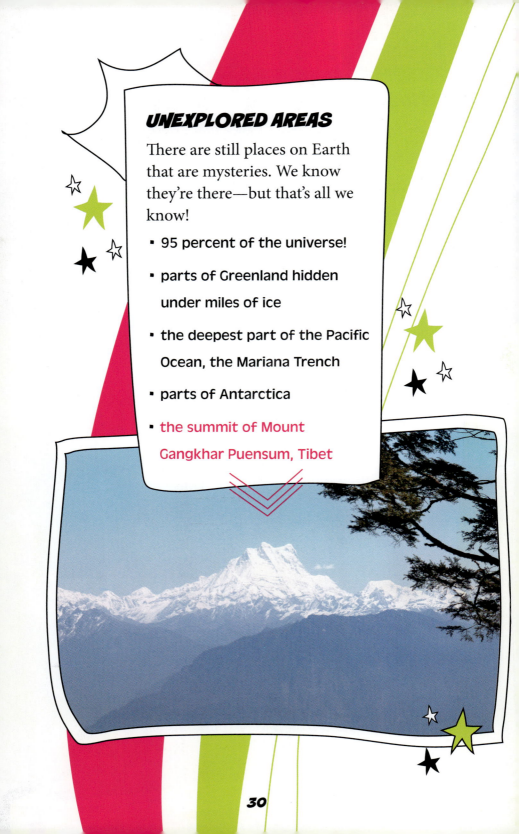

UFO SIGHTINGS

Get out your map. Did aliens stop near you?

- Mount Palomar, California
- North Yorkshire, England
- The Florida Everglades
- Kelly, Kentucky
- White Mountains, New Hampshire
- Roswell, New Mexico
- Holloman Air Force Base, New Mexico
- Chorwon, North Korea
- Skinwalker Ranch, Utah
- Washington, D.C.

MORE INFO FANATIC BOOKS!

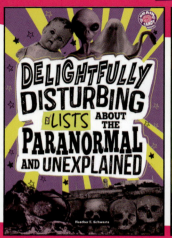
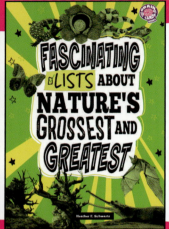
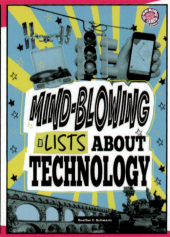

ABOUT THE AUTHOR

Heather E. Schwartz is an author, singer, and performance artist based in upstate New York. She loves writing because she loves learning new things and brainstorming creative ideas. A few sights she would like to see from this book include Cat Island, mammatus clouds, and Prada Marfa. She'd rather not experience spider rain! She lives with her husband and two kids, and their cats, Stampy and Squid.